Introduction:

In January 2007 I started training my dog in obedience. We had a load of fun. After the 8 classes we had learned so much that I thought it would be fun to continue. It was going to be a couple of weeks before the next class started so I just got to playing around. I found an old Hula Hoop in my shed and before I knew it I literally had my dog jumping through hoops. Next came the 1"x6"x10' board and two concrete blocks. Soon I had him jumping over the board, crawling under it, and jumping up and walking across it. So I started looking into Agility training. Honestly, I didn't know much about the sport. I found a great trainer and started classes once per week. I really was having fun with my dog so I wanted to be able to train at home. I looked everywhere, but the equipment was so expensive!! I decided that I could add one obstacle per month. I started with crazy, crude jumps with old 2"x4" boards. I'm not a creative person, or mechanically inclined, or carpentry inclined, I just wanted decent equipment to train my dog and not have to pay through the nose for it. With a lot of effort, a little help from my friends, and a TON of trial and error I now have a whole backyard full of obstacles for my dogs. Yes that's plural now. I adopted a puppy just to add to our fun!! I decided that I could share what I've learned about agility equipment.

First: It can be very expensive, but it doesn't have to be if you build it yourself.

Second: the jumps should be adjustable to accommodate different training levels and different size dogs.

And lastly, safety is important. My first dog walk and jumps were a nightmare and an injury waiting to happen.

What I'm offering is information that can save you a lot of money and time. I have compiled instructions on how to build most Dog Agility obstacles easily and efficiently. Step-by-step instructions that include materials and tools lists. I have way more than $10 in errors in my equipment, and countless hours of effort. I use only materials that are easily available at local Home Improvement Warehouse stores. (I think you know what I mean.) No expensive specialty pieces! Also, I try to make the process simple and each obstacle can be completed from start to finish in about an hour. The instructions include exactly the materials needed for each obstacle so you won't be running back to the store for this piece or that because you didn't think of it. My designs are not all trial regulation, but I have had tremendous success with my dogs and I contribute most of that to the equipment I have.

Instructions included:
Weave Poles
(Stick in the Ground or With a Base)
Adjustable and Versatile Jumps
(Single, double, triple bar, panel and broad configurations possible)
Hoop on Adjustable Stand
Pause Table
Teeter
Dog Walk

Not included are the Tunnel and A-Frame. I tried and tried, and failed for the tunnel, if you need a one, buy one. I also do not include the A-Frame, *it's so BIG!*. With training on the Teeter and Dog Walk my dogs have no problem on the A-Frame. My obstacles are intended to be used for backyard training, supplementing professional training. I make no claim for increased performance from your dog and have no responsibility for injury sustained by you or your dog on obstacles you build using my instructions.

Weave Poles

I know that this sounds too simple to be true but this is exactly how my dogs are trained, and I have awesome weavers.

What you will need:

4 10' lengths of ¾" or 1" PVC
Colored electrical tape (optional)

Tools:
Tape measure
Saw to cut PVC
- A PVC Cutter can be purchased at your local Home Improvement warehouse for about $10. It's well worth the investment for building this equipment.
Hammer

Step 1: Cut the PVC into 3 equal lengths of 40" each.
(Caution! Use care and wear eye protection when cutting PVC.)

Step 2: Find where you want to place them and pound them into the ground. There are a couple of different configurations you can use to start your dog in the weaves. First you can angle the poles left and right. Or you can set the poles a few inches each side of the centerline. Remember that your dog *always* enters the weaves with the first pole on his left. Consult a professional trainer for more tips.

Weave poles are placed 20 inches apart in a straight line. Stripe your poles at 20". This aids in visibility for you and your dog and comes in handy when resetting your poles.

-OR-

Set of 6 Weave Poles with Base

Needed:

3 – 10' lengths of ½" PVC

(I believe this works best, larger PVC is a larger base for the dog to step over.
You can use ¾" to construct the base if you have already used this size for
"stick in the ground" poles, and can save one 10' length.)

11 – ½" PVC Tees (or ¾")

Cut the PVC pipe into the following lengths:

1- 10' pipe into:
    4 – 30" pieces
1- 10' pipe into:
    2 – 30" pieces
    3 – 161/2" pieces
    5 – 2" pieces
(You will have ½" left over.)

1- 10' pipe into:
    4 – 13" pieces
    2 – 19" pieces
    3 – 10" pieces

The 30" pieces will be your poles, put all 6 aside. The remaining pieces will be the base. See color coded diagram below. Construct your base:
First remember that the "side opening" of a Tee is the longer side, the part you could see straight through, and the "center opening" is the shorter side.

Let's start with a Tee. From the center opening push in a 2" piece, and from both side openings push in 13" pieces. Grab another Tee, from the 2" piece attach this **Tee** at a side. (This Tee will face skyward and hold your first pole later)
The next 9 Tee's we will be using the side openings only, and building one long piece.

Push pieces together in the following order:
16 ½" (piece), Tee, 2", **Tee**, 19", **Tee**, 2",
Tee,16 ½" **Tee**, 19", **Tee**, 2", Tee, 16 ½",
Tee, 2", here attach the last Tee using it's
center opening. From the side openings of
this last Tee push in 13" pieces.
The bold "Tee's" in the sequence above
will face skyward and hold the weave poles.
The other 3 will face either left or right and
hold the 10" pieces and act as supports to
make the base more stable. Keeping in
mind that the dog always enters the weave
poles with the first pole on his left turn
these supports to the side that will not
interfere with his feet. (Following the
sequence above the first 10" support will
be to the right and the other 2 will be on
the left.

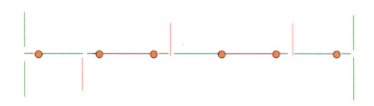

Notice that using the above sequence the dog can enter from either end and still avoid the side supports. If you have a more vigorous dog running through the weaves, here are a couple of suggestions to make them more stable:

Place elbows on the ends of the side supports, including the ends, and add a short length of PVC to be pounded into the ground.

Purchase PVC caps and fill the base with sand. The added weight will add stability.

Remember that when getting started in the weaves a common aid is to "open" the poles by angling them left and right. Open wider to get started and slowly "close" the poles as the dog gets more comfortable weaving. This is easily done with this configuration.
(Gluing some connections is optional, I would recommend trying it out and deciding what will work best for you)

Have Fun!!

Jumps

What you'll need:

I build jumps in sets of 3. This uses the materials most efficiently and offers the most versatility.

4 -10' lengths of PVC pipe
        (I use ¾" but 1" is nice too)
16 Tees (1" or ¾ ", to match your pipe size)
Minimum of 6, ¼" x 2" Carriage bolts and nuts

Tools:
A saw or PVC cutter to cut the PVC pipe
Tape measure
Marker
Drill with ¼" bit

Step 1 – Cut one length of PVC into 3 equal length of 40". These will be your crossbars. (Caution! Use care and wear eye protection when cutting PVC.)

Step 2- Cut one length of PVC into the following lengths:

> 2 – 30" lengths
> 4 – 6" lengths
> 4 – 9 inch lengths

Step 3 – Construct your base by connecting a 6" length to each side of a Tee and a 9" length to that same Tee's center opening. Add another Tee, side opening, to the other end of the 9" length. Connect a second 9" length to the other side opening of that Tee. With the opening in the center of the Tee facing upward when this is placed flat on your work surface you have built your first base.

Step 4 – Repeat steps 2 and 3. When you are finished you should have 6 bases.

Step 5 – With your bases lying flat on your work surface and the opening in the Tee facing upward, connect the 39" pieces. You now have 6 standards.

Step 6 – Carefully measure and mark the height (or heights, see versatility below) that you want your crossbars.   Remove the upright from the base and CAREFULLY dill ¼" holes straight through the PVC upright. (Caution! Use care and wear eye protection when drilling PVC.)
If you drill multiple holes be certain that the holes are in a straight line

and straight through the PVC. Push the carriage bolts through the PVC pipe at the height that you want your crossbars. Hand tighten the nut on the opposite side. The threads should protrude about 1 inch.

Step 7- Reconnect the uprights to the bases with the protruding carriage bolts pointing toward the bottom of the Tee formed by the bases. Slip one open end of a 40" crossbar onto the protruding carriage bolt and the other end of the same crossbar onto another upright. You should have your first jump!!

Do not glue your jumps!!! Press the pieces of PVC together firmly. The jump should collapse easily if collided with to avoid injury!

Repeat this process as many times as need....RUN WITH IT!!

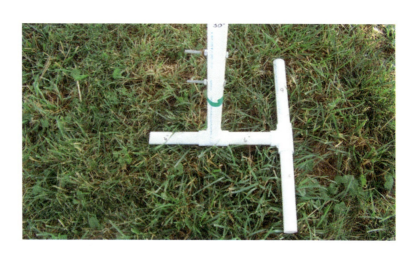

Versatility:

1) To create a double bar jump; place Two jumps side-by side. Remove the 6 inch pieces from the sides of one of the bases and connect it directly to the base of the second jump at the Tee. Reattach your crossbars at the same height.

2) For a Triple jump use a third jump. Reattach your crossbars at ascending heights.

3) For a Broad jump effect use three jumps and place the crossbars low to the ground but further apart. (You can adjust the length of the pieces of the base and connect to jumps together using the PVC Tee's if necessary.)

4) For a Panel jump effect place multiple crossbars on the same set of standards.

Have Fun!!

Hoop

What you will need:

2 – 10' lengths of PVC pipe
(I used 1", 1 ¼" is also a good choice,
Just be certain that the pipe and
connectors are the same size.)
4 – PVC Tees
2 – PVC 90 degree elbows
4 – PVC caps
(optional, see instructions below)

4" corrugated drain pipe
Min 4 – ¼" eye bolts and nuts
Snap hoop to fit eye bolts
String or twine or small cable of your choice
Sand (optional, see instructions below)

Tools:
Saw or cutter to cut PVC
Utility knife to cut drainpipe
Drill and ¼" bit

Step 1:Cut PVC into the following lengths:
(Caution! Use care and wear eye protection
when cutting PVC.)

     4 – 15" each
     2 – 30" each
     2 – 45" each
     2 – 3" each

Step 2: Assemble the hoop stand similar to
the diagram. Start with a Tee. Insert a 15"
length into each side opening. Repeat this
with the other 15" lengths and a second
Tee. From the opening remaining in each
of these pieces connect a 3" length. These
assemblies are your feet. Put aside until
later. Next build a rectangle. The top
corners will be 90 degree elbows and the
bottom corners will be tees. Push the 3"
lengths from the feet into the Tee's from

the rectangle. You should have your hoop stand similar to the diagram.

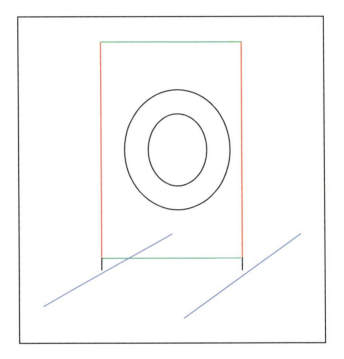

OPTION: Fill the feet with sand and cap with the PVC caps to add weight and stability to your hoop stand.

Step 3: Construct and hang your hoop. The 4" corrugated drain pipe is usually sold in 10' lengths, which have one end tapered with tabs to fit into the next pipe. Cut off about 40" of pipe from the non-tapered end. Bend the pipe around and fit the now cut end into the tapered end. Drill a ¼" hole in the center of the top 30" crossbar from top to bottom. Push an eyebolt through the hole from the bottom up so the "eye" is on the bottom of the bar, secure with a nut. If you don't need an adjustable hoop simply tie the hoop at the desired height.   Loop twine around the sides of the hoop and the frame to keep the hoop in the desired position. To create and adjustable hoop: Attach the snap hook to a length of twine, string or 1/16" cable. Find the lowest desired position and attach that length of twine to the snap hook attached at that first eyebolt. Pull the twine through the eyebolt to the height of the next highest position. Mark on the crossbar where the snap hook should attach to the next eyebolt. Repeat this process until you have all your desired heights. Drill at the marks and attach eyebolts. String the twine through the eyebolts to keep the hoop hanging straight. The loops of twine on the sides should be tight enough to keep the hoop straight but loose enough to allow the hoop to be raised and lowered.

Enjoy your Hoop Jump!

Pause Table

What you will need:

<u>Base #1:</u>
4 – Concrete Blocks

-OR-

<u>Base#2:</u>
2 – 10' lengths of 1" PVC
8 – 90 degree PVC elbows (1")
2 – 1" PVC crosses

Table Top
36"x36" square of Plywood

Hint!! - Many Home Improvement Warehouses sell pieces of plywood other than full 4'X8' sheets. You need only 3'x3'. Look for this size piece and buy only what you need. If it is not the exact size many places offer a cutting service for free (usually 2 cuts). Take advantage of this and take home a 36"x36" table top.

Minimum of 3/8" thickness, ¾" Recommended

1 - 2"x4"x10' Stud
Screws
Paint
Sand

Tools
Circular saw
Screwdriver

Step 1: Assemble Base #1. I didn't see any need to make this complicated. Any dog, any size, can benefit from a simple board on 4 concrete blocks. Your choice to have the blocks lay down for about an 8" height, or stand on end for about a 16" height.

-OR-

Step 1A: Assemble Base #2: For a lighter weight stand you can construct a base using PVC. Cut 8 - 18" pieces; connect an elbow to one end of each.   Create 2 X's by slipping the ends opposite the elbows into the PVC crosses. Position the elbows so that they are opening upward. Now determine the height you would like your table to be. For example, my dogs jump 16", I need a 16" table. Subtract 1" from your height and cut that length for the 4 legs of your table. In my example my legs are 15". Push the legs into the elbows on one X then connect the other X. You now have a PVC table stand.   IF YOU HAVE A LARGER DOG, and thus longer legs, you may find it necessary to add some support to the center of this stand. This is easily done by adding a Tee near the center of the X's on both the top and the bottom and adding legs.   Simply cut the 18" pieces and insert a Tee at the same point on opposite X's.

Step 2: Assemble Table Top. Cut 2"x4"X10' stud into 4 – 30" lengths. (Caution! Use care and wear eye protection when cutting boards.) Screw these pieces on one side of the plywood lining up one edge of the 2"x4" to the edge of the plywood. There will be about 3" between the end of each 2"x4" and the edge of the plywood. Screw down from the plywood into the 2"x4"'s, these pieces adds rigidity and "Stop Boards" to the table.

Step 3: Determine where to set up your table; set concrete blocks about 24" apart in a square and position table top on top. The blocks can be slid out to rest just inside the 2'X4" stop boards. -OR- Position the table top on the PVC Stand. I recommend coating the table top with a mixture of 1 part sand and 2 parts paint. This will not only make your table more weather resistant but accustom your dog to the surface he will come in contact on other Pause Tables.

Sit!   Stay!   (5, 4, 3, 2, 1) Go! Have Fun!

Teeter

What you'll need

<u>Stand</u>
2 – 10'x1" PVC
8 – 1" PVC 45 degree elbows
4 - 1" PVC 90 degree elbows
4 – 1" PVC Crosses
8 – 1" PVC Tee's
2 - 1" PVC caps

<u>Plank</u>
1 -12"x1"x12' plank
4 - 2 hole conduit straps and appropriate
screws to attach it to the plank
1 -¾" x 24" nipple pipe
(or other sturdy pipe to act as a fulcrum)

Sand
Paint
PVC cement

Step 1: Cut the PVC into the following pieces:
(Caution! Use care and wear eye protection when cutting PVC.)
> 12- 8" lengths
> 3 - 13" lengths
> 4 - 12"lengths
> 4 – 4" lengths
> 4 – 6" lengths
> 4 – 2" lengths

Step 2: connect 2 - 2 inch pieces to opposite sides of a cross. Repeat this for a second cross. Cap one 2 inch length on each cross. These pieces will hold your fulcrum and serve as the top of your teeter stand. Put them aside for later.

Step 3: Assemble 2 identical polygon shapes. NOTE: For this step press the pieces together just enough to keep them connected. You will want to disassemble them later to glue them. Working from left to right; Start with one 90 degree elbow with the closed bend to your left and down. Connect an 8" length, and then connect a

Tee from the side opening. Twist this Tee so the opening on the short end faces up, toward the sky, not the top of the shape. Attach another 8" length to the opposite side opening. Next comes a second Tee, this one should be twisted to point away from you, toward what will be the top of the base. Add another 8" length, and another Tee, twisted to point skyward, a fourth 8" length and finally a 90 degree elbow, assembled so that the bend is on the right hand end of the line. This device will be one side of the bottom of your base. Next connect a 4" length to the openings on the 90 degree elbows. A 45 degree elbow comes next, on each side, twisted so that the openings point to the center of the shape. Connect a 12" length to the opening on each 45 degree elbow, followed by another 45 degree elbow on the ends of each of the 12" lengths. These elbows should be twisted so that the openings point toward each other.   From each of these openings connect an 8" length. Complete the top side of the polygon by connecting these 8" lengths with a cross. Between the cross at the top of the shape and the Tee at the bottom of the shape connect a 6" length, a Tee in the center, and a 6" length at the bottom, connected to the Tee that was placed pointing away from you. You should have a shape similar

to the diagram below, with 3 openings pointing skyward. If the shape is not lying flat on your work surface twist the connections until it does.
Repeat the above process to form the opposite side of the base.

8" length
6" length
4" length
12" length
13" length

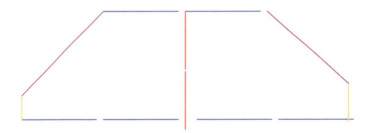

Step 4: You should have constructed two identical polygon shapes with 3 openings. These sides will be connected by the 13" lengths. Firmly press one 13" length into each of the openings on one of the sides. Next fit the opposite ends of the 13" lengths into the corresponding openings on the other side. Stand your base up and assure that it sits squarely on your work surface. You should have two openings on the top of your base.

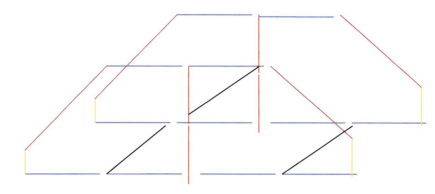

Step 5: Assemble the plank. Measure to find the center of the 12' plank. Attach the 24" nipple pipe (or other sturdy metal bar) to the plank using the 2 hole conduit clamps. You should have several inches of bar extending off the sides of the plank. From these extensions slide on the crosses constructed in Step 2.

Step 6: Carefully insert the non-capped ends of the Crosses from step 5 into the openings in the top of your teeter base. You now have your teeter.

Step 7: The plank on your teeter is slippery. Remove the teeter plank with the Crosses and paint the plank only. Mix 1 part sand with 2 parts paint and coat the plank for traction. This will aid dramatically in training your dog. (Of course you will have to wait for the paint to dry.)

Step 8: You will notice that the teeter base has a tendency to come apart at certain connections. With your PVC cement you can glue your teeter base. I recommend you disassemble the base one side at a time, arrange the pieces so that they are easily reconnected, and glue your teeter base together using the PVC cement manufacturer's directions. Work quickly and be sure all Tee's and other connections are twisted to the correct angle as you work. Do not glue the pivot Tees to the top of the base. This allows the plank to be removed from the base.

Have Fun!!

Dog Walk

What you will need:

<u>Stands</u>
4 -10' lengths of PVC pipe
(I used 1", 1 ¼" is also a good choice
Just be certain that the pipe and
connectors are the same size.)
32 – PVC Tees

<u>Ramps and Plank</u>
2 – 12"x2"x12' boards
1"x2"X10' board
3" hinges
Paint
Sand

Nails
Screws

Tools:
Circular saw to cut PVC and boards
Screwdriver
Hammer

Step 1: Cut PVC into the following
lengths(Caution! Use care and wear eye
protection when cutting PVC and boards.)
        24-8" each
        8-20" each
        8-12" each
Cut *One* of the 12' boards in half at a 45
degree angle. (2 pieces of 6')

Cut the ends of the other board at 45
degree angles, keeping as much length as
possible.

Cut the 1"x2" board into 12 lengths, 10"
each.
 Step 2: Assemble 4 rectangle shapes similar
to the diagram.
Start with 2 tees; connect them with a 20"
length from the center opening. Push an
8" length into one side opening on each

tee. Add another tee, side opening, to each 8" length. Turn these tee's so the center opening is pointing skyward when this piece is lying flat on your work surface. Next comes 8" lengths from each tee, side openings, and another set of tees. This set should be turned so the center openings are facing each other, connect these openings with a 20" length. From   the final opening in this set of tees connect an 8" length, capped off with more tees, with the center openings skyward. You should have a rectangle similar to the diagram. Repeat this process 3 more times for 4 rectangles.

8" length
20" length
12" length
PVC Tee

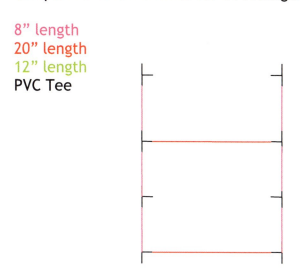

Step 3: With the 12" lengths you will connect 2 rectangles to assemble 1 stand. With one rectangle lying flat on your work surface push one 12" length into each of the openings on the 4 tees. Position a second rectangle over the opposite end of the 12" lengths and press the two sides together. Repeat this process with the remaining pieces for the other stand.

NOTE: This assembly will produce a stand approximately 30" high. This coupled with 6' ascending and descending ramps produces an experience similar to a 48" competition obstacle. For training purposes the length of the 8" pieces can be shortened early in training and lengthened later, utilizing the same ramps and plank. (Concrete blocks can be used early on also for a lower stand)

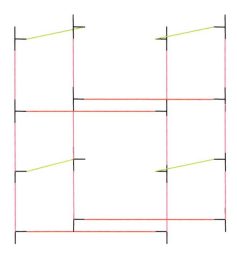

Step 4: Assemble the ramps and plank. The side of each board that is slightly longer than the other due to the angle of the cut will be referred to as the top. Line up all 3 boards end to end, top up. Connect the ramps to the plank with the hinges, being certain the hinges will allow the ramps to fold onto the top of the plank. Nail the pieces of 2"x1" to the ramps tops to create treads. Start about 6 inches from one end and space them about 8 – 10 inches. Coat the top surfaces with one part sand and 2 parts paint for traction.

| | | | | | _____ | | | | |

Step 5: Now that you have your two stands and Plank/Ramps you're ready to put them together. Find flat, level ground and place the stands about 8'   apart. The plank will fit between the four tees on the top of the stands resting on the 12" lengths. I keep the hinged joint of the ramp/plank about 2" from the edge of the stand. This may need adjusting each time the obstacle is repositioned. Test for sturdiness and have a run!!

Option: This whole stand can be eliminated. Cinder blocks can be used for lower dog walks, saw-Horses can be used for higher ones. The disadvantage of these is the weight. The stands described above are lightweight and easily moved. With sawhorses the legs can be made short at first and as the dog(s) gain experience the legs can be made longer.

Note: If you have built the Teeter Stand and have some of the PVC cement left over it's not a bad idea to go ahead and glue the Dog Walk stands together. Follow the manufacturers' instructions for best results.

Enjoy your equipment! I hope that the information provided was helpful. I make no claim to increased performance from you or your dog and cannot be held liable for any loss or injury sustained by your participation in building or using this equipment.

Whether your goal is to create a fun activity for you and your dog or to train for sanctioned Agility trials, I hope this information is helpful.

Run Fast, Run Clean, but most importantly...

Have Fun!!

Made in the USA